Object-oriented Quality and Risk Management (OQRM)

A practical and generic method to manage quality and risks

Peter W.M. van Nederpelt

First edition January 2012
Second edition August 2012
Printer: Lulu Press, Raleigh, N.C., USA.
Translation from Dutch into English: GS Translations, The Meern, The Netherlands.
Editing: English Editing, Rotterdam, The Netherlands.
Author: ir Peter W.M. van Nederpelt EMEA EMIA RO
Author's picture: Dennis van Dijk, www.mooiopdefoto.nl
Design figure 1: Maarten Emons
Publisher: MicroData, Alphen aan den Rijn, the Netherlands
This work uses the publications of Statistics Netherlands as reference. These publications describe earlier versions of the model (Van Nederpelt, 2008 and 2009).
ISBN 978-1-291-037-35-7

Content

Preface

The Object-oriented Quality and Risk Management (OQRM) model emerged out of the search for a management model of quality for the Dutch central bureau of statistics, i.e., Statistics Netherlands. The impetus for this search was the fact that Statistics Netherlands aims to manage quality in a more systematic way in order to comply with the European Statistics Code of Practice.

The search included a study of the quality models: EFQM/INK (2003/2004), ISO 9001, the Balanced Scorecard (Kaplan, 1996), and the Dependency and Vulnerability analysis (A&K 1998), which is a Dutch model. This last model is applied in the context of the Dutch Civil Service Data Information Security Decree (VIR, 2007). The COSO ERM (2004) and ISO 31000 (2009) were added to the list of models later.

When examining the existing models, it has become apparent that these have several disadvantages, such as: complexity, inability to meet internal burdens, and an unclear and inadequate scope.

This was the reason for searching for a new model that could be created out of the existing models; one that does not contain the abovementioned disadvantages. Eventually, this idea led to the creation of the OQRM model. In appendix 3, the relationship between the steps of the OQRM model and the existing models is set out.

Peter van Nederpelt
Alphen aan den Rijn
The Netherlands

Website www.oqrm.org
E-mail info@oqrm.org

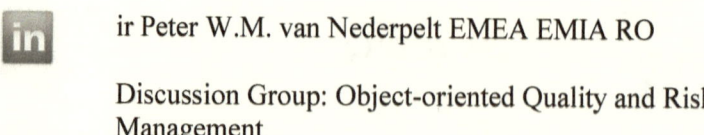

in ir Peter W.M. van Nederpelt EMEA EMIA RO

Discussion Group: Object-oriented Quality and Risk Management

f Peter van Nederpelt

Page: Object-oriented Quality and Risk Management

t OQRMmodel

You Tube OQRM Channel: www.youtube.com/user/pwmvannederpelt

Part I

1	Introduction
2	Area of application
3	Starting principles of OQRM

1.   Introduction

Management wants to do something about quality or risks, but it often does not know where to start. Preferably, the task or the project should not be too complex, nor should it take up too much time, but it must make sense. Moreover, management would like to start with small steps and possibly build on them at a later time. Many managers feel the need for this kind of planning.

The Object-oriented Quality and Risk Management (OQRM) model also seeks to meet this need. This book provides a description of the OQRM model. Its purpose is to enable managers to apply the model in their organization. The model has a number of characteristics which are summarized below:

- Generic. The model can be applied in all organizations, at all levels and in every field of expertise.

- Customized. The model is aimed at the development of frameworks for customized quality systems, either or not using parts of existing models that offer standard solutions.

- Definition. The areas that require management will be clearly defined. How this is done, will be explained later on.

- Scale. The model may be applied on every scale. The user will choose how many and which areas he/she wishes to manage.

- Integration of quality and risk management. There are various methods for quality management and various methods for risk management. However, none of these models integrate quality and risk management, but there is a need for this.

- Systematic. Measures to manage quality or risks are determined systematically.

- Efficient. There is no need to take unnecessary steps or to comply with unnecessary demands. The user will choose the steps that are relevant to his or her situation by himself/herself. For instance, it is not required to provide an overview of all processes in advance.

- Connection with the subjective experience of management. Within the model, other than the management slang, there is very little jargon used. Only the terms of focus area and object are specifically defined within the OQRM model and these cannot be determined intuitively.

Figure 1 summarizes the OQRM model in one illustration.

Reader's guide

This book is made up of four parts and 20 chapters. The first part introduces the reader to the issues and the problems which are central to this work. Chapter 1 is a general introduction. Chapter 2 describes whether OQRM can be applied in a worthwhile manner in your organization. In chapter 3 the basic principles of the model are outlined.

Part II goes into the definition of the area that requires management. The concept of focus area is explained here, a concept which has a central role in the model. It is recommended to look closely and study this first, before reading the following parts.

Part III provides a description of how to systematically determine the right measures to maintain or gain control of the chosen focus areas. The focus area *temperature of coffee* from the coffee machine serves as an example here.

Part III describes a number of examples for applications of the OQRM model in practice.

Appendix 1 contains a glossary. A reference list is incorporated in appendix 2. In appendix 3, the link is made between the steps of the OQRM model and other models. Appendix 4 contains a list of attributes whose purpose is explained at a later time. The same applies to the list of focus areas in appendix 5.

In appendix 6, the list of measures is illustrated. In appendix 7, there is a detailed example of all possible steps that may be taken for the focus area *temperature of coffee*. The book is concluded with a note of thanks.

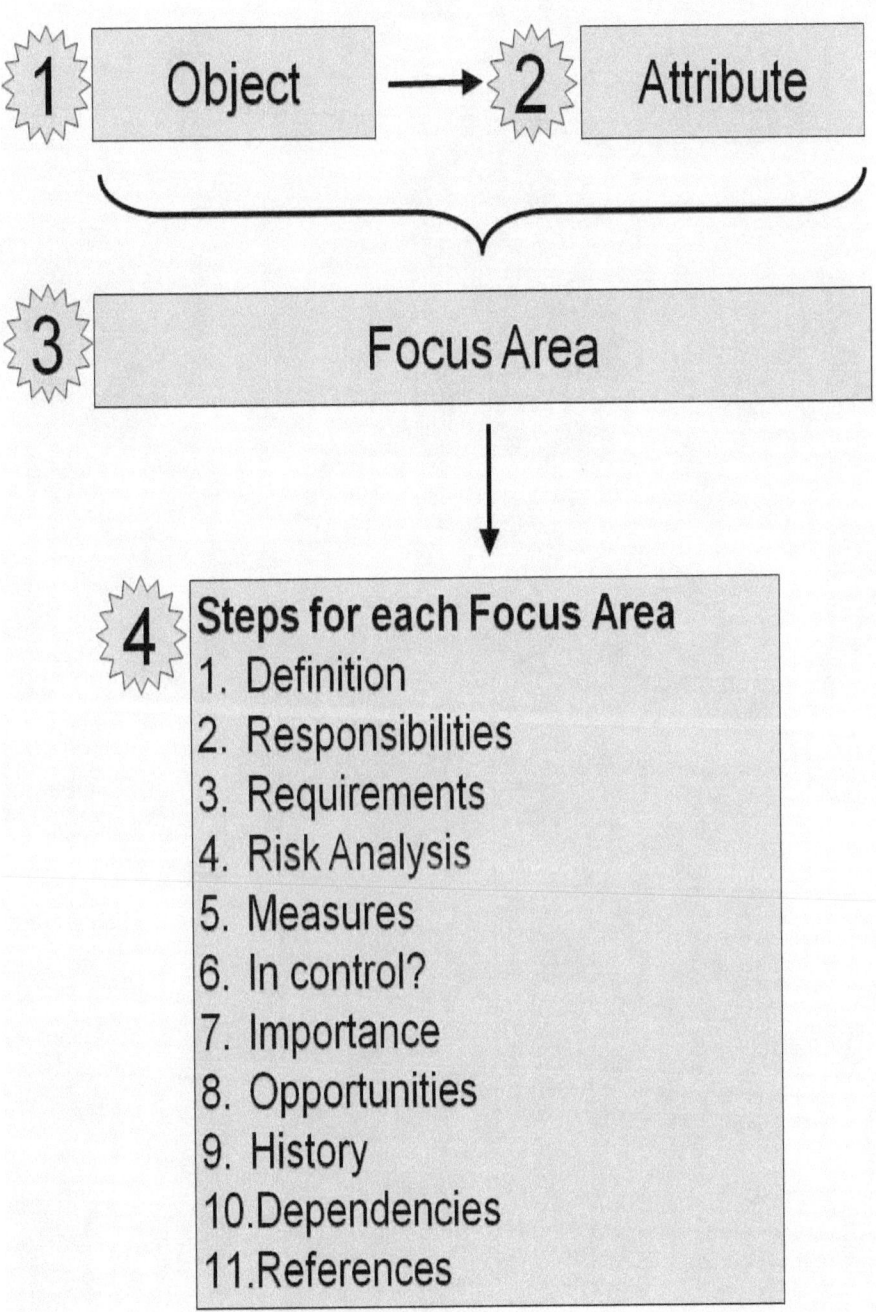

Figure 1 The OQRM model at a glance.

2. Area of application

In this chapter, the area of application of the OQRM model is discussed in detail, so that it may be determined whether OQRM is suitable for your situation.

An important characteristic of the OQRM model is that it may be applied in every organization, at every level, in every field and on every scale. The model is generic in the way it is set up, so it is applicable at all times. The question therefore is why it is not the optimal model in all cases.

The answer to the question above may be the following. If existing models such as ISO9001 and EFQM meet the standards of your organization, it will not be efficient or effective to apply OQRM.

The models referred to contain a list of demands and points requiring attention, respectively. If these demands are applicable to your organization, if they do not contain unnecessary requirements and they provide sufficient coverage, then these models provide a more efficient and cut-and-dried solution. This is a standard solution, which may be effective.

If certification is required, OQRM will not be the right choice either. Certification is not possible with OQRM, nor will it ever be as it is of little use. The model is aimed at customization, rather than at standard solutions.

However, the models which were referred to are not designed for partial application. These are 'all or nothing' models. The OQRM model, on the other hand, provides the user the choice of determining the scope by him/her-self, from small to very large.

The following are a number of examples where OQRM was successfully applied. These are all cases where more customization is required and where existing models do not, or else do not fully, comply with the demands.

1. Putting together a system of standards where multiple existing standards are integrated.
2. Managing the most important risks of the organization.
3. Drawing up a list of requirements for a new website.
4. Drawing up evaluation criteria.
5. Taking measures for improvement of an existing website.

6. Taking stock of the most profitable measures of improvement.
7. Structuring a checklist for self-assessment.
8. Putting together an approach for quality assurance for all primary processes of the organization.
9. Comparing two existing frameworks.
10. Adjusting a control model.
11. Quality of reports on the Internet
12. Conceptual framework quality statistical output.

The abovementioned applications are worked out in part III. There it will become clear how the model is applied in various situations.

The question that may be asked is why OQRM is always applicable. The answer is that the model is 'empty'. This means that it does not contain any knowledge of any field whatsoever. It is more of a method, an approach, and also a way to manage quality and risk in a systematic manner.

There are more models in this category of empty models, such as COSO ERM (2004), the Balanced Scorecard (Kaplan and others, 1996) and ISO 31000 (2009). However, COSO ERM was set up with limited purpose. The Balanced Scorecard has little structure. Moreover, ISO 31000 is only concerned with risk management, but it combines well with OQRM.

Models such as ISO 9001 (2000) and the EFQM Excellence model (EFQM, 2003) are indeed filled. These models have little structure, but contain a lot of knowledge of a certain field in the form of demands, recommendations, and points of attention or norms.

OQRM is rich in structure, but on the other hand, contains no knowledge. It is a tool, which in most cases may be used when it comes to managing quality and/or risk (table 1).

With a bit of good will, one might say that it is a management model in which quality and risk management are integrated. Apart from the points of attention which are referred to in chapter 3, this is a value-free model.

Table 1 Position of OQRM in relation to other quality and risk models.

		Knowledge	
		No	**Yes**
Structure	**Little**	The Balanced Scorecard	ISO 9001
			EFQM
			INK
	Much	COSO ERM	(Dutch) A&K-model
		ISO 31000	
		OQRM	

3. Starting principles of the OQRM model

The OQRM model has the following starting principles:

- An organization is a system of mutually dependent objects. The quality of these objects requires management.
- Quality is a broad concept.
- The organization knows what is good for it.

Organization as system of objects

An organization is a system of mutually dependent objects (Deming, 2000):

"A system is a network of interdependent components that work together to try to accomplish the aim of the system. A system must be managed. It will not manage itself."

William Edwards Deming is speaking of components here, where we use the term objects, but we mean the same thing.

It must be added that the quality of these objects also requires managing. This does not only concern the quality of the object final product, but also the quality of all objects that contribute to the production of these final products. Final products do not hold the monopoly on quality.

The OQRM model assumes that quality and risks may be controlled and improved by taking measures ('control paradigm').

Broad and concrete definition of quality

In 2010 the simple question "What is quality?" was posed in one of the discussion groups on LinkedIn. It resulted in over one hundred most varying responses.

What this boiled down to was that most definitions referred to the quality of the final product of an organization or the satisfaction of the users. Definitions such as 'fit for use' and 'according to the specifications of the customer' were often mentioned.

If, however, the quality concept is vague or too restricted, it will also be difficult to manage. At least, then you do not know what you are managing. The concept of quality will need to be made clearer in relation to the quality of coffee.

It is safe to say that the most important attributes of coffee are temperature, color, odor and taste. These attributes determine the quality of the coffee. From this, the following definition of the concept of quality is derived.

Definition: Quality is the set of attributes of an object

What an object is perceived to be is discussed in chapter 5.

Organization knows what is good for it

Application of the OQRM model requires knowledge of the organization. The model in itself does not contain knowledge of organizations or fields of expertise; it is merely an evaluation tool. The organization itself fills in the empty model provided by OQRM.

Part II: Determine scope by way of focus areas

4	Focus areas
5	Objects
6	Attributes

In this part the terms focus areas, objects and attributes are explained further. These terms are necessary to define the field you, as the manager, wish to manage.

4.   Focus areas

4	Focus areas
5	Objects
6	Attributes

In order to manage quality and/or risks, it is important to determine the area that requires managing (scope). The OQRM model uses the term focus areas for this purpose.

> Definition: A focus area is a combination of an object and one accompanying attribute.
>
> In short: Focus area = Object + Attribute

An example of a focus area is efficiency of a process. The object here is *process* and the attribute is *efficiency*. Other examples of combinations of objects and attributes are:

- Process + duration.

- Employee + competence.

- Information system + availability.

- Customer + satisfaction.

- Report + readability.

- Coffee + temperature (see figure 2)

In appendix 5 various examples of focus areas are given.

The focus area concept plays a central role in the OQRM model. It is a unit that can be managed by taking the right measures. For instance, the focus area *efficiency of a process* may be improved, among other things, by avoiding double or unnecessary activities.

It takes precision to put together a focus area in accordance with the definition. The further steps (part II) are tuned to this.

Focus areas are the building blocks for quality and risk management. Another metaphor is that the focus areas are the backbone for a quality and risk management system. They are also referred to as the stepping stone. These are the areas the user of the model wishes to place in the spotlight.

It is desirable to define the fields that management wishes to manage. After all, you cannot eat the elephant all at once; you need to take one bite at a time. The area that must be managed may be chosen as large or as small as possible according to management's wishes (scalability).

Auditors use the concept of focus areas to define their audit, but they often use a different term for this, which is scope. The scope consists of a combination of objects and accompanying aspects. The term audit variable is also used here.

Defining is not a strongpoint in existing models. A rough outline is considered sufficient, resulting in a loss of precision.

The concept of focus areas also makes it possible to identify differences and similarities (overlaps) in scope between various applications of the OQRM model. For instance, it may so happen that the focus area *competence of employees* is addressed in different ways within the organization, such as, in an audit and in a periodic management report. In this way, different applications of the model may be linked to each other.

A focus area also defines the area where focus is desired. After all, it is not possible to manage everything at the same time. A collection of focus areas may be chosen, for example, from small (one focus area) to large (thirty).

The fact that the attributes of objects can be discussed extensively is a linguistic phenomenon. The OQRM model utilizes this phenomenon. It is possible to set demands on focus areas and carry out a risk analysis for each focus area. A focus area always provides a homogenous and coherent set of control measures. This is what is remarkable about focus areas, as this is not the case with other regulation criteria.

Measures also differ strongly for each focus area. Managing the *efficiency of a process* requires other measures besides managing *integrity of employees*. This even applies to focus areas referring to the same object, such as: *competence of employees* and *mobility of employees*.

Efficiency of processes may be a focus area, efficient processes are not. The first expression does not entail a value assessment; it is a neutral expression. But the second expression does entail a value assessment. Efficient processes do not need to be managed anymore, the efficiency of processes does.

Critical Success Factors (CSF's) may be considered as focus areas that are of vital importance for the organization. Focus areas may further be selected when formulating visions, missions and objectives.

Focus areas may be hard in character such as efficiency in processes; they may also refer to softer matters such as *commitment of employees to the organization* or the *openness of the culture*.

Finally, the concept focus area is domain dependent. Focus areas may be chosen from the most varying fields such as marketing, production, purchasing, automation, finance, personnel, housing, research, health, security and business continuity.

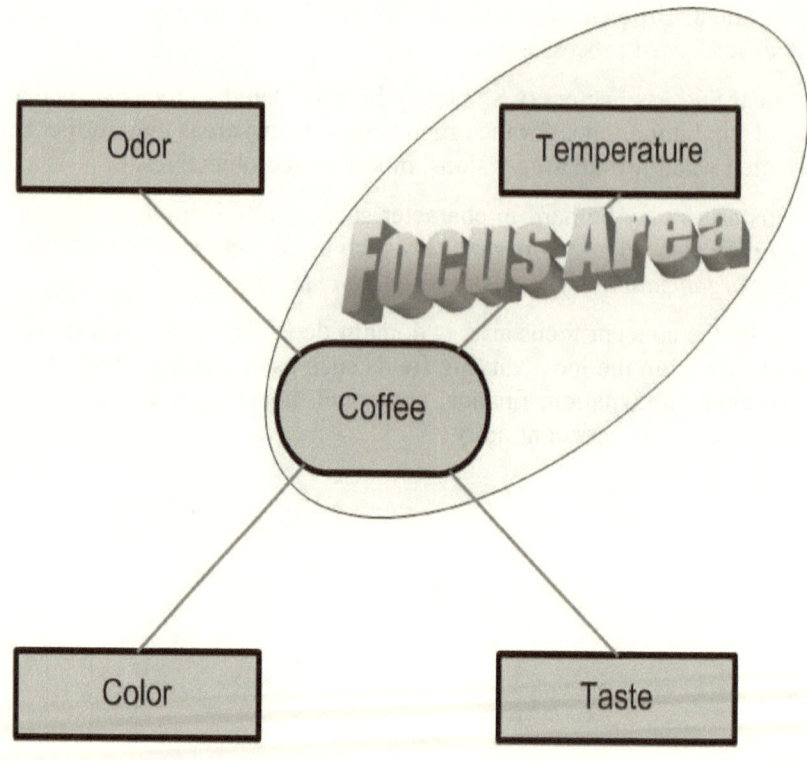

Figure 2 Four focus areas surrounding the 'object' coffee

In the following two chapters, we will go into further detail on the concepts object and attribute.

5. Objects

4	Focus areas
5	**Objects**
6	Attributes

An organization and its environment contain many objects. An important object is the final product or the service that the organization provides, but there are more objects in it that can be named.

Examples of other objects are processes, raw materials, employees and information systems. There are also relevant objects outside the organization, such as customers, suppliers and other parties involved, such as, shareholders and supervisory officials.

More abstract terms, such as, vision, collaboration, identity and culture may also be called objects. Furthermore there are products, such as, reports, strategy, policy and invoices that can be considered as objects. There are small objects, such as file names and large objects, such as the organization as a whole.

The definition of an object is as follows:

Definition: An object is something that has attributes.

In the literature on quality management we not only find the term object, but also terms, such as, object type, component and entity. But this is just a matter of providing a name for something.

Another definition of an object is: Everything that can be perceived or conceived (ISO, 2004). So it does not take much for something to be an object.

An object is always a noun. One rule of thumb is the following. If you can place the expression "the quality of ..." in front of it, you have an object.

An object may be specialized. An example of a special type of *document* is an *offer*. What is notable is that an *offer* has all the attributes of a *document*. In this context, we can speak of an inheritance of attributes. Both a document and an offer have the attributes *correctness, completeness and clarity.*

Objects which may be chosen can be large, such as the object *personnel,* but you may also choose a sub collection such as *management* or the *customer service employees.*

Sometimes you need to split up the objects into related objects. The object *report* may for instance be divided into the following related objects: *set of reports, the structure of the report, the content of the report, the report as document or file, the drafting of the report* and *the publication of the report.* These are objects that belong to the family of the object *report.*

6.   Attributes

4	Focus areas
5	Objects
6	**Attributes**

In this chapter, the meaning of attributes is described.

We can think of many attributes. Certain attributes are easy to measure, such as, temperature, weight, size, costs and duration. This kind of attribute is called a primary quality.

Other attributes exist only in our mind, i.e., secondary quality. Here we refer to attributes such as availability, accessibility and efficiency. This type of attribute is not always easy to measure directly.

Attributes often end on "–ness" or "-ty". Appendix 4 contains a list of attributes which are mostly drawn from management literature.

It must always be possible to standardize an attribute. This means that in combination with an object an attribute may be described as good or bad. The attribute must also be manageable; otherwise the attribute will be irrelevant in the framework of OQRM.

The OQRM model is not fastidious with the use of the term attribute. Attributes such as capacity, duration, efficiency and costs are attributes of objects. Perhaps these attributes are not always associated with quality, but in the OQRM model there is no effort made to distinguish between the attributes that either are or are not associated with quality. This distinction is not relevant for managing an organization.

Certain attributes are relatively vague, if they are not defined. Notorious examples of this are the attributes, such as, reliability and transparency. This is especially the case, when these are not mentioned in combination with an object.

Other attributes are basic, such as, the attribute presence or availability. An object must always be present, for it to be meaningful to attribute things to it.

An attribute is often an adjective or an adverb from which a noun is derived, such as:

1. available → availability
2. honest → honesty

Sometimes going from an adjective or an adverb to a noun is a bit more difficult, such as:
- comfortable → comfort

If you cannot find the right word for a certain attribute, then a last resort may be to describe the attribute, starting with *"the extent to which..."*. For instance, one might say, *the extent to which a handbook is applied* or *the extent to which a procedure is carried out.*

Attributes must be formulated positively, therefore, rather than a word such as, *falseness*, we ought to use the word *authenticity* or *genuineness*.

Part III: Steps for each focus area

7	Definition
8	Responsibilities
9	Requirements
10	Risk analysis
11	Measures
12	In control?
13	Importance
14	Opportunities
15	History
16	Dependencies
17	References

In this part, there is a short description on which steps may be taken for each focus area. Each step is worked out in a separate chapter. The six most important steps for each focus area are:

1. Definition of a focus area. Define what the focus area means.

2. Distribution of responsibilities. Determine who is responsible for the focus area and how it is delegated.

3. Requirements for each focus area. Formulate requirements which the focus area must comply with.

4. Risk analysis for each focus area. Formulate existing and expected problems with the focus area. Analyze possible causes for the problems with the focus area. Determine the possible consequences of problems with the focus area.

5. Measures for each focus area. Determine which measures have already been implemented. Determine which measures are still in progress or have been planned and which measures are yet to be taken.

6. In control. Determine whether management is in control of the focus.

Less important steps are:

7. Importance of the focus area. Determine how important the focus area is for achieving the objectives of the organization.

8. Opportunities in every focus area. Determine which chances the focus area offers for the organization.

9. History of the focus area. Determine what the history of the focus area is.

10. Dependencies on other focus areas. Determine what relationships there are with other focus areas.

11. References for each focus area. Determine which references there are on the focus area.

None of these steps are obligatory. Basically, the order is not prescribed either, but there are logical links between the steps.

- When developing frameworks, requirements must be formulated (step 3).

- In case of quality assurance, determining measures is unavoidable (step 5) and it is obviously also required to determine who will be the responsible party (step 2).

- In order to determine whether the organization is in control (step 6), the requirements must be clear (step 3), the risk analysis must be carried out (step 4) and it must be clear which measures have already been taken (part of step 5).

- In order to carry out a cause and effect analysis on the risk analysis (step 4) it may be useful to examine the relationship with other focus areas (step 10).

- Applying the OQRM model basically comes down to filling in the matrix in table 2. The user him/herself will determine which parts of the matrix are relevant for his/her application.

In part III, the focus area *temperature of coffee* is delineated as an example in every chapter.

Table 2 Matrix of steps and focus areas

Nr	Steps	Focus area 1	Focus area 2	Focus area 3	Focus area 4	Focus area …
1	**Definition**					
2	**Responsibilities**					
3	**Requirements**					
4	**Risk analysis**					
5	**Measures**					
6	**In control?**					
7	Importance					
8	Opportunities					
9	History					
10	Dependencies					
11	References					

7. Definition of a focus area

7	Definition
8	Responsibilities
9	Requirements
10	Risk analysis
11	Measures
12	In control?
13	Importance
14	Opportunities
15	History
16	Dependencies
17	References

You may choose a definition yourself, but this may also be obviously looked up in the literature.

A definition of a focus area often starts with the words "the extent to which ...". This is not the case with directly measurable attributes, such as, weight, duration and volume. For instance, the definition of the weight of an object is the amount of heaviness of that object.

Defining focus areas is only necessary, when what is meant by a focus area is not trivial. Sometimes the meaning of a focus area can be explained in more than one ways. In that case, whatever management wishes to manage precisely, is ambiguous, and this is unacceptable.

The focus area *integrity of employees* may, for example, be defined as the extent to which employees comply with certain legislation in the field of integrity. But integrity of employees may also be defined as the extent to which employees maintain general or professional and ethical norms and values.

The first definition is more concrete, therefore easier to manage, but it is not necessarily better. The person who is in control of the focus area will determine which definition is applicable.

It may sometimes also be necessary to define the object.

Example

Definition of coffee

A beverage made of water and coffee beans which may be dispensed from a coffee machine.

Definition of the temperature of coffee.

The measure of the warmth or coldness of the coffee when it is dispensed from the machine.

8. Distribution of responsibilities for each focus area

7	Definition
8	**Responsibilities**
9	Requirements
10	Risk analysis
11	Measures
12	In control?
13	Importance
14	Opportunities
15	History
16	Dependencies
17	References

In this chapter, the distribution of responsibilities for each focus area is described.

It may sometimes be necessary to point out who is responsible for a focus area. This especially applies when we need to find out whether the company is in control of a focus area and/or if measures are required to gain control.

There are a number of different terms which may be used for the person who is primarily responsible: owner, portfolio holder and initiator.

Responsibilities may be delegated. There may be other parties involved, besides the primarily responsible person. Every person involved has a certain partial responsibility which may be specified further. This responsibility may continue on to the level of employee.

To apply the OQRM model, it is not necessary to have the processes of the organization set out. In order to be able to assign the responsibility, it is only necessary that the organizational structure is known. The responsibility may then be placed on a role or position in this organizational structure. Clearly, for various reasons it is very useful to have the processes of the organization in view.

Example

Distribution of responsibilities for the temperature of coffee from the coffee machines

The Facilities Department leases the coffee machines.

The supplier is responsible for maintenance and solving malfunctions of the machines.

The service engineer will carry out maintenance and solve malfunctions. Users may report malfunctions to the supplier via the Internet.

9. Requirements for each focus area

7	Definition
8	Responsibilities
9	**Requirements**
10	Risk analysis
11	Measures
12	In control?
13	Importance
14	Opportunities
15	History
16	Dependencies
17	References

In this chapter, the requirements for each focus area are described.

Requirements may be determined both in words (qualitatively) as well as in numbers (quantitatively). Quantitative requirements are formulated in norms with supplementary target values. For instance, the duration of the order process may last no more than 3 days.

Requirements may be determined externally, for instance, by legislation and regulations. Furthermore, requirements may be derived from frameworks or standards which you chose yourself or which are common within the branch of industry.

It is possible that decisions made by management in the past refer to a focus area. Finally, the manager of the focus area may as yet formulate requirements him/herself when working out the focus area.

Sometimes requirements are specifically formulated in the shape of required measures. In other cases, a more general formulation is chosen.

If a focus area fails to comply with the requirements, this will be considered a problem with the focus area. This term will later be used during the risk analysis.

Finally, goals of an organization or department may be formulated as a focus area with an accompanying requirement. For instance, productivity of the organization must rise by 2% a year. The same applies to the (key) performance indicators.

Example

Requirements that are set for the temperature of coffee

The coffee must always be at 82 degrees Celsius with a 2 degree margin, when it is made. Odors will then dissolve well. Above this temperature, bitter alkaloids will also dissolve and below this temperature the coffee will be tasteless, colorless and odorless.

10. Risk analysis for each focus area

7	Definition
8	Responsibilities
9	Requirements
10	**Risk analysis**
11	Measures
12	In control?
13	Importance
14	Opportunities
15	History
16	Dependencies
17	References

This chapter describes the step where the risks within a focus area are set out.

The risk analysis has three elements:

- Problems with the focus area

- Possible causes of problems with the focus area

- Possible consequences of problems with the focus area

These elements will be discussed in detail further below. In general we can state that the risk analysis adds two aspects, namely, the cause and effect aspect and the aspect of working with uncertainties.

> Definition: Risk is the effect of uncertainty on objectives (ISO, 2009).

Problems with the focus area

If a focus area does not meet the requirements, then there is a problem with that focus area. A problem may, in fact, already present itself or be expected in the future.

Possible causes of problems with the focus area

Other words for possible causes of problems with a focus area are threats or vulnerabilities.

The reason for reporting possible causes of problems with a focus area is that measures may be taken to reduce these causes or to thwart them with preventive measures.

Possible consequences of problems with the focus area

Other words for consequences are effects or impacts. The reason for formulating possible consequences of problems with the focus areas is that measures may be taken to soften the consequences with curative measures.

Risk level

If the effect is multiplied by the chance of this problem occurring, the risk level may be estimated. Risk level is also known as the extent of the risk and risk valuation.

Risk level = Chance x Effect

One suggestion is to express the chance on a scale from 1 to 5, and the effect as well:

1 = zero to very small

2 = small

3 = reasonably small

4 = big

5 = very big to 100%

The risk level may assume the values from 1 to 25.

Gross risk

There may be a distinction between gross and net risk. With gross risk, there is no regard for measures already taken. The gross risk may be relevant, when selecting focus areas from a list of candidates. Gross risk is also called inherent risk.

Net risk

Net risk is also known as residual risk. With net risk, there is regard for the measures already taken (step 5). Determining the net risk is relevant in order to find out whether the organization is in control (step 6).

Chain of consequences

There may be a chain of consequences: the consequences of the consequences. For example: problems with the completeness of a contract with a customer may lead to misunderstandings between parties. Misunderstandings may lead to loss of trust. Loss of trust may lead to loss of turnover, and therefore, financial damage.

You may also indicate which consequences you are actually worried about or interested in. These, for example, may be: only financial damage, or consequences for the quality of the final product, or dissatisfied customers. In this way, the chain is restricted at the same time. Here we are concerned with the consequences for the objectives as these are recorded in the definition of risk.

ISO 31000

ISO 31000 (2009) is designed for risk management and combines well with OQRM. Just like OQRM, it is an empty and generic model. It contains no knowledge of any domain whatsoever. The added value of the OQRM model is the concept of focus areas, where the scope of risk management is made explicit.

Example

Risk analysis for the temperature of coffee

There is a *problem* with the temperature of the coffee, when it is not at about 82 degrees Celsius. Currently, this problem does not occur.

Possible causes of problems are that the temperature of the water in the water reservoir is not set correctly, or that parts may be damaged.

Possible consequences of problems with the coffee temperature are complaints from the employees. The coffee is too tepid or too hot. Moreover, the coffee will not taste or smell very well and the color of the coffee will not be in order.

The *chance* that there will be a problem is low (1 on a scale of 5). The machine undergoes maintenance and is tuned regularly. Furthermore, the parts of the machine are reliable.

Moreover, if the *effect* is small (1 on a scale of 5) and should the problem occur somehow, then an employee can always walk to another machine.

So the *level of the residual risk* is small: $1 \times 1 = 1$.

11. Measures for each focus area

7	Definition
8	Responsibilities
9	Requirements
10	Risk analysis
11	**Measures**
12	In control?
13	Importance
14	Opportunities
15	History
16	Dependencies
17	References

This chapter is about designating measures for each focus area.

Types of measures

We can distinguish four types of measures:

- Signaling measures
- Preventive measures
- Curative measures
- Mitigating measures

In case of signaling measures, there will be set of indicators, whose values may be measured. If a target value is exceeded, a signal is given.

Preventive measures prevent problems from occurring with a focus area.

Curative measures may remove, reduce, or absorb the consequences of problems with a focus area.

Finally, we have the mitigating measures, which are measures that transfer the risks to other parties.

In the risk analysis, both the possible causes and possible consequences of problems with the focus area are laid down. This may be used when determining the appropriate measures.

We will choose the focus area *fire safety of a building* to illustrate how the four types of measures work. First we will take preventive measures by the application of prescriptions for this area. For example, one measure is to apply fire-resistant materials.

In case there is a fire, curative measures may be that fire-extinguishers are set in place in the building and that there is a telephone number to report a fire alarm. An evacuation plan is also a curative measure.

A signaling measure in this case is that there are smoke detectors installed in the building, which will give a signal as soon as there is emission of smoke or when a certain temperature is exceeded.

A mitigating measure is that the building is insured against fire. Damages, if any, will then be covered by the insurer.

Stages

Furthermore, we may make a distinction between the stages that measures are carried out:

1. Implemented measures. These measures are already in force and have already been implemented.
2. Measures in progress or planned measures. These measures are not yet fully implemented. The organization is still working on them, or is yet to start them.
3. Additional measures. These are extra measures, or measures yet to be planned, which are to be taken in order to sufficiently control a focus area.

In order to determine whether an organization is currently in control, it is necessary to know which measures have already been taken (point 1). In order to determine whether the organization will be in control in the future, it must also be determined which measures are in progress or planned (point 2). Subsequently, it may be determined whether additional measures are required (point 3).

When drafting a plan for further control of a focus area all measures that have not yet been implemented are open to consideration (point 2 and 3).

Finally, we may look at some possible measures. Here, we may use best practices within the branches of industry. However, we do not need to re-invent the wheel, when determining any additional measures.

Simons

Simons (1995) has made a subdivision of four categories of measures:

1. Diagnostic Control System
2. Belief System
3. Boundary System
4. Interactive Control System

When determining the appropriate measures, you may keep these types in mind. The question is which type is most effective in a given situation.

These categories of measures are characterized below. Here a system is looked upon as a set of measures.

Diagnostic Control System (detection system)

Measures in this category ensure that reaching important goals is guaranteed, and that there are no deviations. It keeps KPI's within boundaries which have been agreed upon. It also provides feedback for readjustments. Managers use these systems to compare planning and realization. It is the cockpit of the organization.

Belief System (convictions)

Measures in this category empower the employees and encourages them to seek new possibilities. It also communicates core values. Moreover, it inspires workers to commit themselves to the goals of the organization. It puts value in model behavior of management. Therefore, it must be broad enough to appeal to all employees. It is always expressed in the mission of the organization.

Without a belief system, employees will not have a clear picture of the core values of the organization and they will operate based on assumptions. A belief system may inspire workers to develop new ideas. It functions as the sun, the warmth and the light (yang) and it breeds involvement.

Boundary system (frameworks)

Measures in this category contain the rules of the game. It points out actions and pitfalls that workers should avoid. It is the direct opposite of Belief Systems. It draws dark and cold boundaries (yin). It is contained in the codes of conduct and the codes of ethical behavior. It covers what is not allowed. It shows workers there is no blank check. It also serves as the brakes of the organization. Moreover, it points out risks that are to be avoided. It is also linked with sanctions and it provides protection against possible opportunist behavior.

Interactive Control System (interaction with the surroundings)

Measures in this category set out opportunities and threats. It gives the top management team the possibility to react proactively. It leads to renewal on all fronts. It also challenges management to analyze the changing surroundings.

It is the subject of discussion of strategic management. It keeps an eye on uncertainties of a strategic nature. Moreover, it is about changes in technology, customer needs, legislation and regulations and competition. It may also change future plans and forecasts. It may also be used to further analyze unexpected success.

Measures as objects

Measures are also objects themselves, so we may speak of the quality of measures. For example, the *competence of employees* may be increased by *training*. Subsequently, we may speak of *effectiveness of the training*. Which measure to take depends on what management would like to shed a light on and what the desired level of detail of the management process is.

Example

Measures to control the temperature of coffee

One measure that has been taken is the conclusion of a maintenance contract. Moreover, more machines are installed in the building (mitigating measure). Furthermore, on the Internet the customer can gain access to the supplier to report malfunctions.

Additional measures are not necessary, because the organization is in control. See step 6.

---

12. In control?

7	Definition
8	Responsibilities
9	Requirements
10	Risk analysis
11	Measures
12	**In control?**
13	Importance
14	Opportunities
15	History
16	Dependencies
17	References

This chapter provides a description of the way in which it is determined whether a focus area is in control, or else sufficiently controlled.

Being in control means two things. On the one hand, the requirements set must be complied with. On the other hand, the extent of the residual risk must be acceptable. If neither of these two is met, it means that the organization is not in control and extra measures will be required.

We may also find that too many measures were taken. But the organization would then also gain control through less measures. In that case, measures may be withdrawn.

Being in control may be looked upon in two ways. On the one hand, we might say that a focus area is in control, because all the necessary measures have been implemented, but are also in progress and/or planned.

It is also possible to have a stricter view and say that the focus areas are not yet in control, as long as not all necessary measures have been fully carried out and completed. After all, as long as measures are in progress or planned, there are currently risks that are being run.

The follow-up question is: *when* is a focus area indeed in control? This is when all necessary measurements have been carried out in full.

In order to carry out an improvement cycle, this step needs to be repeated periodically. We then speak of 'continuous improvement'.

Example

Is management in control of the temperature of the coffee?

The requirements are complied with according to the logbook of the service engineer and the history of malfunctions.

The residual risk is acceptable, because its level is low.

We conclude that the organization is in control of the focus area. There are no additional measures necessary.

---

13. Importance of a focus area

7	Definition
8	Responsibilities
9	Requirements
10	Risk analysis
11	Measures
12	In control?
13	**Importance**
14	Opportunities
15	History
16	Dependencies
17	References

This chapter discusses the determination of the importance of a focus area.

Determining the importance of a focus area is necessary if a choice must be made between focus areas, or else priorities must be set.

There are many ways to determine the importance of a focus area. On the one hand, this may be done in a subjective manner. Someone then more or less intuitively determines the importance of the focus area. On the other hand, this may be objectified by putting the question to more people and then taking the answers that are given most often (modus).

Furthermore, there are criteria that we can think of for the extent of the importance. A criterion for determining the importance may be the level of the residual risk or net risk. Focus areas with the highest residual risk will then receive primary attention.

Another criterion in determining the importance of a focus area is the extent of the inherent risk or gross risk. In determining the risk here, the measures already taken are disregarded. These are the focus areas with the highest risk level, in case no measures have been taken.

> **Example**
>
> **Importance of the temperature of coffee**
>
> The importance is low. The focus area has hardly any influence on reaching the goals of the organization, namely, the quality of the final product and/or the satisfaction of the customers.

14. Opportunities for each focus area

7	Definition
8	Responsibilities
9	Requirements
10	Risk analysis
11	Measures
12	In control?
13	Importance
14	**Opportunities**
15	History
16	Dependencies
17	References

Opportunities are the counterpart of negative effects. If a focus area is in control, it may also offer opportunities for the organization. If the *efficiency of an organization* is larger than that of the competition, this will lead to lower prices of the products and in turn, possibly an increasing market share.

Example

Opportunities for the organization regarding the temperature of coffee

The temperature of coffee provides no opportunities for the organization.

---

15. History for each focus area

7	Definition
8	Responsibilities
9	Requirements
10	Risk analysis
11	Measures
12	In control?
13	Importance
14	Opportunities
15	**History**
16	Dependencies
17	References

A focus area may also have already been at the centre of attention in the past, possibly under a different name. There may be a need to describe this past in order to place the focus area in a historic context.

In the past, there may also have been successes or failures with a focus area. This may also be relevant to know in order to subsequently take into account.

Example

History of the temperature of coffee
The temperature of the coffee has always been in order over the past 12 months.

---

16. Dependencies of focus areas

7	Definition
8	Responsibilities
9	Requirements
10	Risk analysis
11	Measures
12	In control?
13	Importance
14	Opportunities
15	History
16	**Dependencies**
17	References

Focus areas rarely stand alone; they often depend on other focus areas. Examples are:

- The *costs of a product* are dependent on the *efficiency of the production process* and the *costs of the raw materials.*

- The *customer-friendliness of the organization* depends on the *adequacy of the procedures* that customers have access to and the *competence of the employees* who must carry out those procedures.

An analysis of dependencies on other focus areas may help with the risk analysis. In the last example, inadequate procedures may cause problems with the *customer-friendliness of the organization* and then measures might be taken to revise the procedures.

Table 3 Example of a semantic network

Focus area	Dependency	Focus area
The adequacy of customer procedures	influences	the customer-friendliness of the organization
The competence of employees	also determines	the customer-friendliness of the organization.

It is possible to create a semantic network of focus areas. This means that dependencies between focus areas may be created where the type of dependency is also defined. See table 3.

Example

Dependencies of the temperature of coffee on focus areas

Problems with the temperature of the coffee have consequences for the satisfaction of the employees and for their productivity.

The temperature of coffee also has an effect on the taste, the odor and the color of the coffee.

---

17. References for each focus area

7	Definition
8	Responsibilities
9	Requirements
10	Risk analysis
11	Measures
12	In control?
13	Importance
14	Opportunities
15	History
16	Dependencies
17	**References**

There may already have been some things written about a focus area. This may be in the form of notes, books, reports, articles, plans, logbooks, and minutes of the meetings of the board of directors. In this step the types of reference involved are laid down, resulting in a reading list.

Example

References of the temperature of coffee

Contract with the supplier.

Handbook for the service engineer, including checklist for maintenance and check-up.

Maintenance plan for the machine.

Logbook of the service engineer.

Malfunction history.

Part IV: Examples of applications

18	Frameworks
19	Quality and risk management
20	Other applications

In this part examples of applications of the OQRM model are worked out.

18. Frameworks

18	Frameworks
19	Quality and risk management
21	Other applications

This chapter contains examples of the drafting of or the integration of frameworks. A framework is defined here as a collection of demands, criteria, guidelines, prescriptions, points of attention, and principles or recommendations.

Integration of frameworks

The organization had to comply with various frameworks (legislation and regulations, guidelines, codes of conduct, and adopted resolutions). This was unclear for all parties involved.

These frameworks were integrated by determining the focus area of every requirement. Afterward, these requirements were arranged according to the focus area. The integrated framework was hierarchically structured with objects at the highest level, focus areas beneath that and requirements set for each focus area.

All requirements were then explained; the sources of these requirements were also stated, along with a description of the possible consequences in case of failure to comply with a requirement.

The result was a clear and easily maintainable system of standards, due to its unambiguous structure.

Comparison of two frameworks

Two organizations wanted to compare their frameworks to determine the differences. These differences were discussed between the two parties for the purpose of bringing these two frameworks closer together.

For this, the focus areas for all the formulated requirements in the frameworks were also determined. Subsequently, for each focus area it was checked if a statement was made. There were two possible situations: both frameworks made statements, which were different from each other, or one of the frameworks did not produce a statement on this.

No discussions were required in the focus areas where both frameworks made comparable statements. For the rest of them, a discussion was indeed worthwhile.

Requirements website

The task force responsible for a website for a specific target group wanted to determine which requirements should a website meet.

In regards to the website, focus areas such as the *relevance of the publications* were formulated. Subsequently, explicit requirements were set for these focus areas. For example, the publications had to be interesting for a wide group of users.

Evaluation criteria

The organization wanted to check whether reports to the outside world were capable of improvement. A pilot was carried out with an improved form of these reports. This pilot needed to be evaluated.

A distinction was made between various objects here, such as the guidelines for the reports, the reports themselves, the process of drafting the reports and the pilot project.

For the focus area *clarity of the reports*, the evaluation criterion (requirement) was that according to the assessor the report had to be understandable and interesting to read.

Conceptual framework quality statistical output

In an organization, there were various references for the quality of statistical output. The knowledge of this was fragmented. A decision was made to assemble all knowledge on statistical output and add to it where it is necessary.

All attributes of statistical output were set out. Apparently there were 19 of them, so there were 19 focus areas surrounding the object statistical output.

Each of these attributes was defined. Furthermore, it was checked which requirements were set on a general level and what would be possible causes and effects of problems with this attribute. Eventually the indicators for the attributes in question were set out.

It also appeared that the object statistical output required further distribution. A distinction was made between the data, the statistical concept (among which definitions of variables) and the output as reference or file, the explanation of the statistical output and the supply of the figures.

This resulted in a conceptual framework, and consequently, a basis for other references regarding the quality of statistical output. The focus areas that were found are listed in table 4.

Table 4 Focus areas surrounding the object statistical output

Focus area	
Object	**Attributes**
Data	Accuracy Availability. Comparability (in the time and between domains) Comprehensiveness Confidentiality Consistency Indisputability Plausibility Reliability Reproducibility Validity Verifiability
Statistical concept	Relevance Completeness Coherence with other statistics.
Explanation	Clarity
Reference or file	Accessibility
Supply of the output	Timeliness Punctuality

Not all attributes exclude each other. There are great similarities, for instance between accuracy and reliability. The same applies to consistency and plausibility.

Framework for reports on the Internet

The organization had the intention to further improve the reports on the Internet. At first, the attributes which might be identified with such reporting were set out.

It became clear that the object reporting required further specification. This led to the following partial objects: set of reports, the format of the structure or the report, the content, the drafting process, the report as product and the time of publication (release) of the report.

This research resulted in the attributes and focus areas, respectively, which can be found in table 5 (Van Nederpelt, 2011).

Table 5 Focus areas surrounding the object reporting

Focus area	
Object	**Attribute**
Set of reports	Completeness
Structure	Conformity to existing standards
	Relevance
	Adequacy
	Completeness
Content	Consistency
	Clarity
	Unambiguousness
	Correctness
	Language
	Transparency
	Completeness
Reporting as product	Familiarity
	Usability ('usability on Internet')
	Accessibility
Drafting the report	Duration
	Costs
Publication of the report	Timeliness
	Punctuality

Subsequently, for each of the attributes requirements were set from the viewpoint of the users. For example, concerning the duration, it was required that the report would have to be drafted within six weeks.

Within the framework that was set, the improved version of the reports was implemented.

19. Quality and risk management

18	Frameworks
19	**Quality and risk management**
21	Other applications

In this chapter, the applications that refer to quality and risk management are described. This means that the measures to control the chosen focus areas are also dealt with.

Primary risk areas

The board of directors felt the need to determine the most important risks of the organization and to take any additional measures to reduce these risks to an acceptable level.

Through a brainstorm guided by a process supervisor, the board determined which focus areas had the highest residual risk. It also determined who would be the portfolio holder of each focus area and who else would be involved.

The quality department then developed these focus areas further and answered the following questions:

- What is the history of the focus area and has there been any attention directed to it earlier?
- What are possible causes and effects of problems with this focus area?
- Which measures have been taken, are in progress or have been planned?
- What possible measures are there?

The portfolio holders first reviewed the report from the quality department and adjusted this where necessary. Then they themselves determined whether any additional measures were necessary. They also drafted a plan of action for all measures which were not yet carried out in full.

Each quarter, the progress of the plan of action is reported in the regular planning and control cycle. It has been agreed that this whole exercise will be repeated annually.

Most profitable improvement measures

One department wanted to check out which improvement measures would be necessary to take in the field of quality and what kind of priority this should have.

In an afternoon workshop, the most important improvement measures were determined in three steps. In the first step, the objects relevant to the department were determined.

The second step saw attributes linked to these objects, resulting in a list of focus areas.

Management made a selection of the most important focus areas. In the third step, the participants worked out the areas which were worthy of attention in groups of 4 to 5 persons, carrying out the following steps:
- Defining the focus area.
- Formulating requirements regarding the focus area.
- Determining possible causes and effects of problems with the focus area.
- Setting additional measures based on the previous steps.

After the workshop, management drafted a plan of action based on the latter measures. This plan of action was subsequently executed.

Quality assurance of the primary processes

The organization wanted the quality of all primary processes to be guaranteed (quality assurance) by taking the right control measures. Some of the measures were taken on the level of the organization, but others were specifically meant for the process in question.

For each process, a quality reference was drafted. Standard contents of this reference were a description of the process, both graphically and textually, and also a list of information systems that support the process.

For a standard set of focus areas, it was determined by the owner of the process what its relevance to the process was and which requirements could be set for that purpose.

Examples of these focus areas are:
- Precision of the input
- Availability of employees
- Confidentiality of the data

- Soundness of the methodology
- Availability of information systems

Based on this analysis measures were specified for the process. The types of measures involved were standardized here. The elaboration on these measures was process-specific. Examples of this are:

- Authorisation procedure
- Plausibility check
- Agreements with customers and suppliers, both internally and externally
- Production planning
- Version control
- Operating instructions
- Handbooks
- Incidents and calamities procedure

The whole process was supported by a handbook with explanations and complete instructions, a set of templates and assistance from a member of staff, if necessary. As there are a large number of primary processes, everything was standardized as much as possible. The quality reference will be updated every year for the most important processes, and every three years for the other processes. The periodic process of updating will be subject to central planning and the progress will be monitored.

Improvement measures website

The department responsible for the website of the organization felt the need to determine what would be the most important points of improvement regarding the website.

A large number of people involved in the website were invited to a workshop. In this workshop, first a list of focus areas (48 in total) was drafted through brainstorming. From this list, management selected the twelve most important ones.

Then six groups worked out two focus areas per group. First they defined the focus areas, then they determined which requirements would have to be set for these focus areas. They also determined for which possible causes and effects of problems with the focus areas, there would be (risk analysis). Finally, they formulated possible measures.

Later the quality department added possible measures to the list of measures which also fit in with the requirements set and with the risk analysis. For each requirement, each cause, and each effect, a measure could be found.

After the workshop, management made a selection of the measures that should have priority. Progress of the execution of these measures will be monitored annually through an audit.

20. Other applications

18	Frameworks
19	Quality and risk management
21	**Other applications**

This chapter contains a description of other applications that are interesting too.

Control model

The organization was looking for an improved structure for the periodic management reports to the board of directors. The existing reports contained bottlenecks regarding the primary processes, HRM, finance and a list of KPI's. Moreover, there were appendices in which the progress of special subjects was dealt with, including actions which were discerned from an organization-wide risk analysis.

It was proposed to choose focus areas as the main structure and categorize all subjects under them. This proved quite possible. The structure of the report become much clearer because of it and it also became more apparent what the scope of the report was. As a result, it was easier to determine which areas could be left out and which were still lacking. Finally, even the size of the report was reduced, while its content was maintained.

Self-assessment

The quality department wanted to find a good structure for a self-assessment questionnaire. In order to make the self-assessment transparent for the user and moreover, to make it easy to maintain for the quality department, it quickly needed to become clear what the scope of the self-assessment was.

The self-assessment was given a hierarchical structure with objects as its highest level, followed by focus areas. For each focus area, one or more requirements were formulated as questions.

Furthermore, for each focus area, it was formulated how the person completing the questionnaire measured the residual risk: acceptable or not acceptable. If the residual risk was not acceptable, the question was asked, which additional measures would then be desired.

Longlist, shortlist

The quality department felt the need to draw a list of possible focus areas for the organization. This list would serve as input for all possible projects in the field of quality and risk management.

The quality department analyzed 15 strategic references. It was checked which focus areas were named in these references. These focus areas were placed in a database with quotes from the references. This resulted in a long-list of focus areas supplemented with information which was already known about these focus areas. The result was a list of approximately 300 focus areas.

Representatives from throughout the organization assessed the importance of each of these focus areas. This way, the focus areas could now be arranged in sequence of importance and a shortlist could be drafted.

Both the shortlist and the long-list are used to check whether any focus areas have been overlooked.

Appendices

Appendix 1: Glossary

This appendix contains the definition of terms used in this book.

Table 7 Terms

Term	Definition and remarks
Focus area	Combination of an object and one accompanying attribute. *See appendix 5 for examples.*
Gross risk	Possible consequences with <u>no</u> regard for measures already taken.
Attribute	Capacity of something. *See appendix 4 for examples.*
Inherent risk	See gross risk.
Framework	Scope within which one can or must remain. *For instance by setting or formulating requirements*
Quality	The set of attributes of an object
Quality management	Managing attributes of objects (focus areas) by taking measures.
Net risk	Possible consequences, keeping into account measures already taken.
Management	See quality management.
Object	Something that has attributes.
Residual risk	See net risk.
Risk	Effect of uncertainty on objectives (ISO, 2009)
Risk management	Managing possible causes and possible consequences of problems with attributes of objects (focus areas) by taking measures.
Risk level	Chance x effect. The chance here refers to the occurrence of the effect. Furthermore, this is about the effect on reaching objectives.

Appendix 2: References

ABD (2003). *Competency management.* (Dutch) Senior Civil Service.

A&K (1998). (Dutch) Handbook Dependency and Vulnerability analysis. (Dutch) Agentschap Advies- en Coördinatiepunt Informatiebeveiliging (ACIB) - consultancy and coordination agency for information security.

Cannegieter, Jan Jaap **(2001)**. (Dutch) *Kwaliteitszorg in ICT projecten,* the Proqua method - Quality care in ICT projects. Ten Hagen Stam.

COSO-ERM (2004a). *Enterprise risk management.* Integrated framework. Management summary. September.

COSO-ERM (2004b). *Enterprise Risk Management Framework.* Committee of Sponsoring Organizations of the Treadway Commission.

Daas, Piet J.H, and van Nederpelt, Peter W.M. **(2010)**. *Application of the object oriented quality management model to secondary data sources.* The Hague/Heerlen: Statistics Netherlands.

De Leeuw, Prof. Dr. Ir. A.C.J. **(1986)**. *Organisations: Management, Analysis, Design and Change.* Gorcum.

De Leeuw, Prof. Dr. Ir. A.C.J. **(2003)**. (Dutch) *Bedrijfskundige methodologie, management van onderzoek* - Business methodology, management of research. Gorcum, 5th edition.

Deming, W. Edwards **(2000)**. *The New Economics: for Industry, Government, Education.* Cambridge, MA.: MIT Press.

EFQM (2003a). The *EFQM Excellence Model. De overheid- en de non-profitsector.* Brussels: European Foundation for Quality Management.

EFQM (2003b). Assessing for Excellence. *A practical guide for successfully developing, executing and reviewing a Self-Assessment strategy for your organization.* Brussels: European Foundation for Quality Management.

INK (2004). (Dutch) *Handleiding positiebepaling publieke sector onderwijs zorginstellingen* - Handbook on positioning public sector education care institutions. Papendrecht: Triam Kennismanagement.

ISO (**2000**). *ISO 9001:2000. Quality management systems* – Requirements, Delft: (Nederlands Normalisatie-instituut.

ISO (2001). *ISO-NEN/IEC 9126. Information technology – Software product quality.* Delft: Nederlands Normalisatie-instituut.

ISO (2004). *ISO /IEC FDIS 11179-1. Information technology – Metadata registers – Part 1: Frameworks.* Delft: Nederlands Normalisatie-instituut.

ISO (**2005**). *ISO 9000:2005. Quality management systems* – Basic principles and glossary. Delft: Nederlands Normalisatie-instituut.

ISO (2009a). *NEN-ISO 31000. Risk management – Principles and guidelines.* Delft: Nederlands Normalisatie-instituut.

ISO (2009b). *NPR-ISO Guide 73. Risk management – Glossary.* Delft: Nederlands Normalisatie-instituut.

Kaplan, Robert S., and Norton, David P. (**1996**). *The Balanced Scorecard*: translating strategy into action, Boston, MA: Harvard Business School Press.

Muntinga, Drs. Marc A. and Lagerveld, Drs. Niels J. (**2004**). *Managementmodellen voor kwaliteit* - Management models for quality, Kluwer, 2nd edition.

Nijssen, Prof. Dr. Ir. G.M. (2001). (Dutch) *Kenniskunde 1A.* - Epistemology Heerlen: PNA Publishing.

Simons, Robert (1995). *Control in an Age of Empowerment.* Harvard Business Review. March-April.

van Nederpelt EMEA, P.W.M. (**2008**). (Dutch) *Objectgeoriënteerde Kwaliteitszorg, een managementmodel voor kwaliteit* - Object oriented Quality care, a management model for quality. The Hague/Heerlen: CBS.

van Nederpelt, P.W.M. (**2009**). *Creation and application of a new quality management model.* Prague: Paper Conference Statistics: Investment in the Future 2.

van Nederpelt, P.W.M. (**2010**). (Dutch) *Is er nog plaats voor een nieuw kwaliteitsmodel?* - Is there room for a new quality model? The Hague/Heerlen: CBS.

van Nederpelt, P.W.M. (**2011**). *Attributes of Quality Reports.* The Hague/Heerlen: Statistics Netherlands.

Appendix 3: Relations with other models

The OQRM model was composed by first analyzing existing models. Below we provide a step-by-step explanation of the OQRM model, what relationship there is with existing models.

In the analysis of the existing models, these have been stripped of domain-specific knowledge. In epistemology, this process is called making texts *knowledge-independent* (Kenniskunde, Nijssen 2001).

Focus areas

1. The term focus area is identical to the term *scope* as it is applied in the auditing domain. In auditing, the scope of an audit consists of the *object* of research, plus related *aspects*. In OQRM the term *object* is also used, with the same meaning. Instead of *aspect*, in OQRM the term *attribute* is used.
2. EFQM (2003) uses the term *criteria*. This term somewhat resembles the term focus area. However, a criterion in EFQM consists only of an object, without aspect. These criteria are:
   1. leadership,
   2. people,
   3. policy & strategy,
   4. partnerships & resources,
   5. processes,
   6. people results,
   7. customer results,
   8. society results and
   9. key performance results.
   These EFQM criteria have the same function as the focus areas in the OQRM model.
3. The Balanced Scorecard (Kaplan, 1996) has four areas of 'strategic objectives':
   - financial,
   - customer,
   - internal,
   - learning and growth.
   These areas have the same function as the focus areas in the OQRM model.

4. In ISO 9001 the chapter division of the ISO norm has the function of focus areas.
5. The Dutch Dependency and Vulnerability analysis (A&K) (1998) distinguishes the so-called MAPGOOD components: *people, equipment, software, data, organization, environment and services.* All these components have the attributes *availability, exclusivity and integrity* (BEI) linked to them. The A&K-analysis has therefore standardized the focus areas and contains 3 x 7 = 21 focus areas. However, at the centre is the focus area *reliability of information systems.*

Distribution of responsibilities

1. The term 'responsibilities' is generally known in management literature. It is often used simultaneously with the terms tasks and authorities.

Requirements

1. The term *'requirements'* is also used in the A&K-analysis (1996). This specifically concerns requirements of reliability towards information systems.
2. EFQM (2003) sets general requirements for the level of the *criteria* and *sub criteria*. For example: Policy and strategy are (must be) communicated and executed through a framework of key processes (sub criterion 2d). In the EFQM model, these are called points of attention.
3. ISO 9001 also sets *requirements*, although these refer to the measures that must be taken. For example: the organization must determine the order and interaction of processes (4.1.b).

Causes of problems with the focus area

1. The A&K-analysis (1998) is about *threats and vulnerabilities.*
2. COSO-ERM (2004) is about *identifying events.* This is one of eight components of this model.

Consequences of problems with the focus area

3. The term *'consequences'* is also used in the A&K-analysis (1996). If something goes wrong with one of the MAPGOOD-components, what will the consequences be? What will the damage be?
4. COSO-ERM (2004) uses the term *risk assessment.* This is one of the eight components of COSO-ERM.

Signaling measures (indicators)

- *Indicators* are emphatically dealt with in the Balanced Scorecard (Kaplan and others, 1996).
- In the criteria 6 to 9, EFQM mentions the terms *perception measurements*, *performance indicators* and *performance results*. In all cases, this concerns quantifiable variables. According to the EFQM model, the results of the organization must be measurable and be measured in the outside world.

Measures

5. The term measures or control measures is generally known in management literature. COSO-ERM (2004), for example, speaks of *control activities*.
6. The A&K-analysis (1998) gives broad attention to determining measures and testing measures.

Importance of the focus area for the organization

7. The term *importance* is also used in the A&K-analysis (1998). This use, for instance, is about the *confidentiality of data* for the *reliability of an information system.*

Dependencies to other focus areas

8. Dependencies between focus areas appear in the literature about the quality of data. One dependency often mentioned is the relationship between *accuracy of data* and the *timeliness of data*. Drafting accurate data may be done at the expense of their timeliness and vice versa. There is an interaction between the two focus areas.
9. In the A&K-analysis (1998) it is stated that the *reliability of an information system* is dependent on the *reliability of the MAPGOOD-components.*

Opportunities

10. The term opportunities stems from the *SWOT-analysis* (strength-weakness analysis). One of the four components of the SWOT-analysis is *opportunities*. This is the same as an opportunity in this framework.
11. COSO-ERM (2004) also speaks of making use of *opportunities.*

Appendix 4: Examples of attributes

This appendix contains a list of attributes without the associated objects. Most attributes can be found in management literature. The list is not exhaustive. No completeness is implied.

A

Ability to …
Ability to concentrate
Able-bodiedness
Acceptability
Acceptability degree
Accessibility
Accountability
Accuracy
Adaptability
Adaptivity
Added value
Adjustability
Affection
Affinity
Affordability
Aimed towards …
Analyzability
Anointability
Anticipative capacity
Appealing
Applicability
Approachability
Appropriateness
Attainability
Attractiveness
Authenticity
Authority to …
Autonomy
Availability
Avoidability
Awareness

B

Beauty

C

Capability
Carefulness
Changeability
Clarity
Clearness
Coherence
Cohesion
Collaboration-oriented
Collector's item-worthy
Comfort
Comparability
Compatibility
Competence
Competence (professional)
Competitive force
Competitiveness
Completeness
Complexity
Compliance
Comprehensibility
Conceivability
Confidentiality
Congruity
Connection with …
Consistency
Containability
Continuity
Contradictability
Controllability
Coping ability
Correctness

Courage
Coverage (degree)
Creativity
Credibility
Creditworthiness
Customer focus
Customer-friendliness

D

Daring
Decisiveness
Dedication
Demonstrability
Dependency
Depth
Desirability
Discretion
Disputability
Diversity
Divisibility
Downgradable
Duality
Dynamic

E

Ease
Ease of operation
Effectiveness
Efficiency
Employability
Energy
Enthusiasm
Entrepreneurial spirit
Environmental awareness
Environmental friendliness
Equality
Equipment level
Equivalence
Exchangeability
Exclusivity
Expandability
Expertise
Explanatory power

Expressiveness

F

Fairness
Faithfulness
Falsifiability
Familiarity
Fastidiousness
Faultlessness
Feasibility
Fertility
Filling degree
Findability
Fit in-capacity
Flawlessness
Flexibility
Form
Freshness
Friendliness
Full-fledgedness
Functionality
Future-proofness

G

Growth

H

Habitability
Hackability
Health
Helpfulness
Heterogeneousness
Homogeneity
Honesty
Human orientation

I

Identifiability
Image
Immunity to stress
Impartiality
Importance
In concrete terms
Independence

Influentialness
Informality
Initiative
Innovative capacity
Innovativeness
Inspiration
Installability
Integrity
Intensity
Interpretability
Inventiveness
Involvement

J

Justice

L

Lawfulness
Leadership
Learnability
Learning capacity
Legality
Legitimacy
Level
Level-headedness
Liability
Linkability
Loyalty

M

Maintainability
Manageability
Manoeuvrability
Market orientation
Maturity
Measurability
Mobility
Modifiability
Modificational capacity
Motivational capacity
Multiformity
Mutational degree

N

Naturalness
Neatness
Necessity
Negotiability
Network competence

O

Objectivity
Obligingness
Odor
Openness
Operability
Operation
Operational safety

P

Perceptibility
Perfection
Performance
Perseverance
Persuasiveness
Pertness
Planability
Plausibility
Policy relevance
Portability
Potential
Power
Precision
Predictability
Predictive power
Preparedness to …
Presence
Prevalence
Process-oriented
Productivity
Product-oriented
Professionalism
Profitability
Progress
Promptness
Proportionality
Protectability

Punctuality
Purchasing power
Pureness
Purpose
Purposiveness

R

Range
Rareness
Reaction time
Readability
Realism
Reasonableness
Recognizability
Recovery time
Redundancy
Relatability
Relevance
Reliability
Reparability
Repeatability
Replaceability
Representativeness
Reproducibility
Resource behaviour
Resourcefulness
Response rate
Responsibility
Responsibility sense
Responsiveness
Result-oriented
Reusability
Riskiness
Robustness

S

Safety
Sanctionability
Satisfaction
Scientific in nature
Scope
Selectivity
Self-confidence

Self-insight
Sensitivity
Servitude
Shallowness
Sharpness
Shrewdness
Simplicity
Simultaneousness
Sincerity
Single-mindedness
Skilfulness
Speed
Sportsmanship
Stability
Steadiness
Straightforwardness
Strength
Structure
Subsidiarity
Sufficiency
Surveyability
Sustainability
Symmetry
Synergy level

T

Tenability
Tenaciousness
Tendency towards …
Testability
Thoroughness
Thoughtfulness
Timeliness
Topicality
Traceability
Transferability
Transitional rate
Transparency

U

Unambiguousness
Unavoidability
Uniformity

Uniqueness
Usability
Usefulness

V

Validity
Value
Value in use
Variance
Verifiability
Versatility
Visibility
Vitality
Voluntariness
Vulnerability

W

Well-foundedness
Wholeness
Willingness
Workability

Directly measurable attributes (primary quality)

Acceleration
Age
Capacity
Color

Cost-effectiveness
Costs
Delivery time
Dimensions
Duration
Frequency
Height
Length
Life span
Output
Periodicity
Price
Profit
Quantity
Reaction time
Recovery time
Response time
Size
Speed
Turnover
Volume
Weight
Width

Appendix 5: Examples of focus areas

In this appendix there are examples of focus areas. The list serves as an illustration and is obviously not complete. The objects software and employee have separate overviews as these two have a large number of attributes.

Table 8 Examples of focus areas

Focus area	
Object	**Attribute**
Data	Accessibility Availability Completeness Correctness Topicality
Document (piece of text)	Accessibility Clarity Completeness Comprehensibility Conformity with standard Consistency Correctness Readability Unambiguousness
Housing	Accessibility Capacity (Fire) Safety
Income and expenditures	Completeness Legitimacy
IT infrastructure	Accessibility Availability Continuity
Annual accounts	Correctness
Customer	Satisfaction

Focus area	
Object	**Attribute**
Supplier	Continuity
	Reliability of supply
Organization as a whole	Continuity
	Customer-friendliness
	Independence
	Integrity
	Profitability
	Sustainability
Personnel	Availability
	Capacity
Process	Appropriateness
	Complexity
	Duration
	Effectiveness
	Efficiency
	Repeatability
	Robustness
Product	Costs
	Delivery time
	Flawlessness
	Functionality
	Image
	Price
	Sustainability
	Variance towards specifications
Project	Conformity with plan of action
	Duration
	Effectiviness
	Progress
Collaboration	Intensity

Focus area	
Object	**Attribute**
Vision	Balance
	Clearness, clarity
	Completeness
	Continuity
	Credibility
	Extent in which vision inspires
	Extent of implementations
	Familiarity to the employees
	Feasibility
	Operation/effectiveness
Food	Freshness
	Odour
	Safety
	Taste
	Tenability
	Texture

Attributes of software

The attributes of software are specified in ISO 9126 (2001). Six attributes have been developed into 32 sub attributes (Cannegieter, 2001).

Table 9 Examples of focus areas surrounding the object software

Software	
Attribute	**Sub attribute**
Functionality	Accuracy Compliance Interoperability Security Suitability Traceability
Reliability	Availability Degradability Fault tolerance Maturity Recoverability
Usability	Attractiveness Clarity Customisability Explicitness Helpfulness Learnability Operability Understandability User-friendliness
Efficiency	Resource behaviour Time behaviour
Maintainability	Analysability Changeability Manageability Reusability Stability Testability

Software	
Attribute	**Sub attribute**
Portability	Adaptability Confromance Installability Replaceability

Attributes of employees

Employees have attributes, such as, competence. This attribute may be divided into a number of sub attributes (ABD, 2003).

Ability to...
Attainability
Availability
Mobility
Motivation
Preparedness to...
Productivity
Tendency towards...
Vitality

Sub attributes of competence
Adaptability
Analytic capacity
Anticipating capacity
Controlling capacity
Customer focus
Customer-friendliness
Daring
Decisiveness
Dedication
Energy
Environmental awareness
Flexibility in behaviour
Flexibility, conceptual
Immunity to stress
Initiative
Integrity
Involvement with

Learning ability
Network competence
Organizational sensitivity
Performance motivation
Persuasiveness
Purposive-ness
Self-confidence
Self-insight
Sensitivity, interpersonal
Sensitivity, managerial
Task-focused managing
Tenaciousness
Unifying leadership
Vision of the future

Capacity
- to change gears quickly
- to collaborate
- to delegate
- to develop employees
- to form a judgment
- to listen
- to manage organization - oriented
- to monitor progress
- to plan and organise
- to self-develop

Appendix 6: Examples of measures

In this appendix, some samples of measures are given. It should be obvious that this list is not complete, nor can it be.

Action plan
Administrative organization
Agreements
Alarm
Analysis
Announcement
Articles of association
Auditing
Authorities
Benchmark
Check
Checklist
Collaboration
Communication
Conference
Consultation
Contract
Conversation
Core values
Correction
Course
Covenant
Critical success factors
Dashboard
Detection system
Discussion
Documentation
Education
Evaluation
Explanation
Feedback
Guideline
Handbook
Infrastructure
Instruction

IT-systems
Job description
Judgement
Justification
Key performance indicators
Logo
Look-out
Measurements
Meetings
Method
Mission
Monitoring
Newsletter
Plan
Plan Do Check Act
Planning & control cycle
Policy
Power of attorney
Preliminary inquiry
Prescription
Press release
Procedure
Program
Project
Publication
Recruitment
Reference magazine
Regulations
Report
Report
Research
Review
Rules of conduct
Sanctions
Security

Selection
Self-reflection
Seminar
Service Level Agreement
Speech
Staff magazine
Standard
Statement
Strategy
Structure
Support
Surveillance
System

Target
Taskforce
Template
Test
Tone at the top
Tool
Training
Trip
Vision
Website
Work meeting
Workshop

Appendix 7: Examples of specified focus area

In this appendix, all steps from part II are developed, based on the focus area temperature of coffee from a coffee machine (figure 3). It is an overview of the examples already mentioned in the part II chapters.

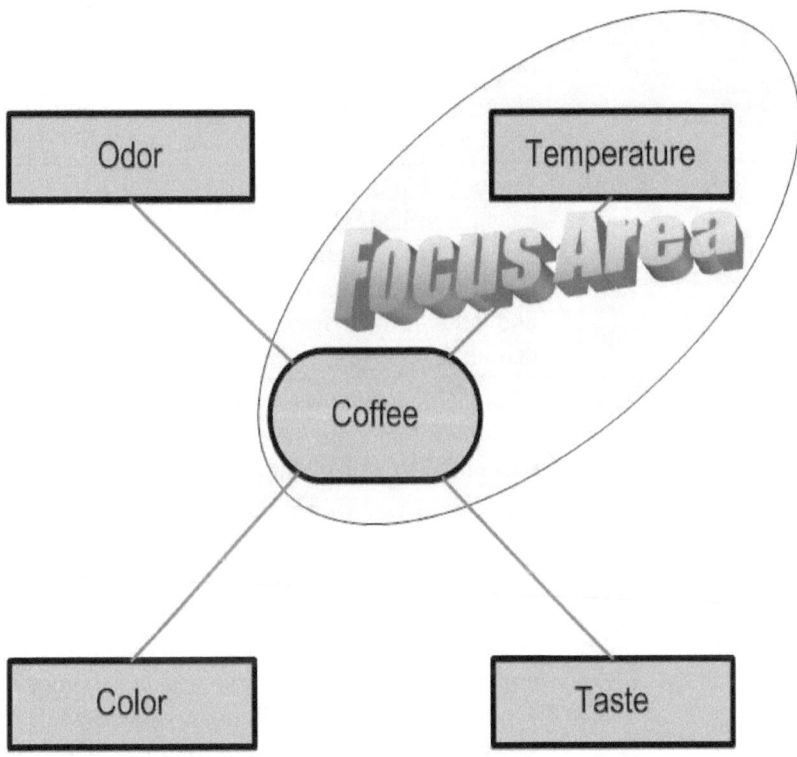

Figure 3 Focus area temperature of coffee

Table 10 Steps worked out for the focus area temperature of coffee

Nr	Step	Specification
1	Definition	The measure of the warmth or coldness of the coffee when it is dispensed from the machine in Celsius.
2	Responsibilities	The Facilities Department leases the coffee machines. The supplier is responsible for maintenance and solving malfunctions of the machines. The service engineer will carry out maintenance and solve the malfunctions.
		Users may report malfunctions to the supplier via the Internet.
3	Requirements	The coffee must always be at 82 degrees Celsius with a 2 degree margin, when it is made. Odors will then dissolve well. Above this temperature, also bitter alkaloids will dissolve and below this temperature, the coffee will be tasteless, colorless and odorless.
4	Risk analysis	There is a *problem* with the temperature of the coffee, if it is not at 82 degrees Celsius. Currently, this problem does not occur.
		Possible causes of problems are that the temperature of the water is not set correctly, or that parts may be damaged.
		Possible consequences of problems with the coffee temperature are complaints by the employees. The coffee is too tepid or too hot. Moreover, the coffee will not taste very well and the color of the coffee will not be in order.
		The *chance* that the consequences will occur is low (1 on a scale of 5). The machine undergoes maintenance and is tuned regularly. Furthermore, the parts of the machine are reliable.
		On top of this, the *effect* is small (1 on a scale of 5), should the problem occur somehow. An employee can always walk to another machine. The level of the residual risk is small: $1 \times 1 = 1$.

Nr	Step	Specification
5	Measures	One measure that has been taken is the conclusion of a maintenance contract (preventive). Moreover, more machines are installed in the building (mitigating measure). Furthermore, on the Internet the customer can gain access to the supplier to report malfunctions (curative). Additional measures are not necessary, because the organization is in control. See step 5.
6	In control?	The requirements are complied with according to the logbook of the service engineer and the history of malfunctions. The residual risk is acceptable, because its level is low. We conclude that the organization is in control of the focus area. There are no additional measures necessary.
7	Importance	The importance is low. The focus area has hardly any influence on reaching the goals of the organization, the quality of the final product and/or the satisfaction of the customers.
8	Opportunities	The temperature of coffee provides no opportunities for the organization.
9	History	The temperature of the coffee has always been in order over the past 12 months.
10	Dependencies	Problems with the temperature of the coffee have consequences for the satisfaction of the employees and for their productivity. The temperature of coffee also has an effect on the taste, the odor and the color of the coffee.
11	References	Contract with the supplier. Handbook for the service engineer, including checklist for maintenance and check-up. Maintenance plan for the machine. Logbook of the service engineer. Malfunction history.

Acknowledgements

The OQRM model was developed thanks to the capacity that the sector Process Development and Quality of the Methodology and Quality division of Statistics Netherlands was able to deploy for this subject. The model was further improved by its application within Statistics Netherlands. Up to now, the model has been applied in fifteen cases, in so far as it is known.

Many employees of Statistics Netherlands have contributed to the development of the model. First and foremost, management provided the opportunity to develop the model; Peter Struijs, in particular, initiated - and strongly stimulated - the search for an adequate quality model. Furthermore, Kees Zeelenberg and Barteld Braaksma fully supported the process of searching and applying.

There were colleagues who commented on the model and others who applied it. Dick Kroeze and Maarten Emons especially come to mind here. Finally, Astrid Kroeze checked the text for errors in style and spelling. I owe them all my gratitude.

Furthermore, I had the opportunity to do research on the quality of the model myself, in the scope of the study Internal and Operational Auditing at Erasmus University in Rotterdam, where I was supported by my guiding counselors Alexander Babeliowksy and Ron de Korte and a group of fellow-students. They reviewed the research report several times.

Then there were a number of people who were prepared to be interviewed in the scope of the research. They contributed important input for the improvement of the model. The interviewees were Huub Vinkenburg, Bernadette van Pampus and Marc Muntinga.

The book was written in the evening hours at home and on the train from home to the office and back. I would like to thank my wife Raphaelle and my daughters Lotte and Tosca for their patience.

Guy Schuitemaker translated the Dutch version of the book into English. Kirsten van Ummersen is native American speaker and edited the book. I am very happy with the result.

Finally, I wish to thank everyone who directly or indirectly contributed to the content and the realization of this book and whose name I have not mentioned here.

www.ingramcontent.com/pod-product-compliance
Lightning Source LLC
Chambersburg PA
CBHW022110170526
45157CB00004B/1565